I0487015

Teamwork

Moving Beyond Teambuilding Exercises

Kenneth McGhee

Outskirts Press, Inc.
Denver, Colorado

Teamwork
Moving Beyond Teambuilding Exercises

Outskirts Press, Inc.
http://www.outskirtspress.com

ISBN: 978-1-4327-1580-9

Outskirts Press and the "OP" logo are trademarks belonging to Outskirts Press, Inc.

PRINTED IN THE UNITED STATES OF AMERICA

Table of Contents

Dedication

This handbook is dedicated to my family, friends, and peers. Thank you for your love, support, and encouragement, which have made my journey through life a great team experience.

Introduction

"Teamwork" is a term that is often used and just as frequently misunderstood. It sounds good for organizational leaders to say, "We are working as a team," or "We have a team approach." However, the reality is that most organizations don't know what teamwork is or how to utilize the concept. Often this term is used to create a sense of cohesiveness. The idea is to help people feel more comfortable and to have positive experiences within the organization.

The word "team," when used in non-athletic situations, has taken on an entirely different meaning. Sports teams typically have a head coach and at least one assistant coach. The coaches share the responsibility of preparing the team for games and other administrative duties. Some team members are selected as the starters, and remaining team members may be assigned to the second team, third team or the practice squad. The roles and responsibilities of each team member are clearly defined, and an effort is made to instill each person with a sense of accountability involving the team's goals.

In a non-athletic organizational setting, the word "team" has sometimes come to mean a sense of getting along with each other. Teambuilding exercises are sometimes used in an attempt to encourage people to interact outside of their everyday organizational roles. In reality, some of these sessions are better defined as stress-reduction workshops. These sessions may also serve as a reminder to relax and not take work and life so seriously.

Reducing stress and striking more of a work/life balance are worthy causes. Although this is true, teambuilding should not start and stop with the utilization of this approach. Staff members also need to be trained, developed, and released to fulfill their roles in an organization.

I decided to write about teamwork based on numerous work and volunteer experiences after seeing the results of organizations that attempted to utilize a team approach without understanding the real dynamics involved. Bitter feelings and increased organizational politics were the end result. Based upon my personal experiences and research, "teamwork" is an easy word to say, but a difficult word to put into practice.

The results of true organizational teamwork are powerful. True teamwork can change an organization, an industry, or society in general. For this reason, it is worth the time to gain a better understanding of teamwork.

Chapter 1: Building a Leadership Foundation

Leadership is at the core of any quality team. Being ethical is important and essential to develop a strong and lasting organization. Trust in relationships is equal to the concrete foundation of a house. You can make the rest of the house look great, but a leak in the foundation will show up in a storm. With ethics being such an essential factor for leaders to consider, why is this element missing in a number of situations?

John Maxwell, in his book *There's No Such Things as "Business" Ethics*, found that five main factors are involved when a leader is tempted to act in an unethical way. These five factors are pressure, pleasure, power, pride, and priorities.

1. Pressure - Organizational culture and management demands were found to be a major source of tension. Enron was also used as an example of people feeling pressure to cook the corporate books.

2. Pleasure – Americans desire to have things exactly when they want them is a contributing issue. Maxwell also discusses the popular phrase, "If it feels good, do it."

3. Power - The abuse of power by corporate executives is discussed. My favorite part from this section of the book is when the author states that power is like drinking salt water: the more you drink, the thirstier you get.

4. Pride - Maxwell considers basic self-confidence to be good, but also believes that an exaggerated sense of self-worth has the ability to destroy a person. Maxwell uses one of John Ruskin's quotes in this part of the book. Ruskin, who was a 19th century writer and art critic, says that pride is at the root of great mistakes.

5. Priorities - Maxwell discusses a question posed to Jim Collins, the author of *Built to Last*, regarding the importance of ethics to the success of the organizations he studied. Collins found that people with good ethics lay a solid foundation for business success.

Clearly, understanding what others are saying is also important. Stephen Covey, in his book *The Seven Habits of Highly Effective People*, makes this point when he says that few people are trained in how to listen effectively. From the time we are children, reading and writing are seen as important. Listening is seen as falling into these four categories:

1. Ignoring a Person - This is when you are not listening when another person is speaking.

2. Pretending - Faking responses to another person.

3. Selective Listening - This takes place when you only hear certain things being said by someone else.

4. Empathic Listening - The goal is to clearly hear and see what is being said. Covey makes the point that this is not a technique like active listening or reflective thinking; rather, it is an effort meant to truly hear the other person.

Covey makes a point about communication. Character affects how people hear, listen, and react to your words. Influence is seen as a reaction to a leader's character.

Organizational History

Do you know your organization's history? If not, you are missing a large part of the puzzle. Does the current structure match up with the original intent of the organization's founders? Listening to the stories of long-term organizational employees and members inside and outside of your department is important. Ask yourself the question "Why are you telling me this?" Please also consider the below questions:

- Is the organization fiscally sound?

- What is the average length of employment among current managers?
- What is the average length of employment among current employees?
- What is your industry's opinion of the organization?
- What is the political climate of the organization?
- Is a union and/or civil service system in place? If so, do you have experience working or supervising in this type of environment? If not, what type of research will make you more knowledgeable about this type of environment?

One Important Question

A point comes when you are considering or have already decided to take a leadership role in an organization. Knowing the answers to organizational history questions is important before making a final decision on how to proceed. One important question to consider is: **"Will I be allowed to lead?"**
Are you the first person to hold a newly created position? If so, what is the philosophy of the person who offered you the position or who hired you? If you are replacing someone else, why is the position currently open? Does the organization have a history of hiring people and allowing them to put new ideas in place? Are any current employees applying for the position? Will you be asked to supervise someone who applied for the position? Have you been informed that addressing long-term challenges

will be a part of your role, and if so, do you feel comfortable with the explanation given to you for why the long-term challenges still exist?

Some organizations will hire an employee perfectly suited to tackle the tasks at hand. Due to the politics of the organization, you might not be allowed to lead. If you find yourself already in this type of dynamic, take lots of notes; you will learn a lot about what should be done. This experience will be very valuable when a genuine opportunity to lead presents itself.

No organization is perfect, and all organizations have their challenges. The key is determining whether your skills and approach make a good match for the organization's approach and culture related to the tasks at hand.

New Organizational Positions

Understanding organizational history and how to deal properly with the politics is a key to success. You should start the process during your interview preparation and the interview itself for a leadership position. If you do not learn this lesson, future promotional opportunities may be severely limited. In some cases, a committee of administrators is involved in the job interview process. Some of these administrators may appear interested in hiring you, but you may have to answer a set of additional questions to satisfy the concerns of the other members of the interview committee. They might also require a second level interview.

Below are some questions to ponder when considering the position and shortly after accepting a new organizational position:

- What is the history behind the creation of the position?
- How long was the process behind getting the new position approved?
- Is there any known resistance to the creation of the position?
- Does the position require the employee to perform job tasks that someone else should be performing?
- Who will be, or who is, the supervisor, and does the organizational reporting line make sense based upon organizational structure?
- What former and/or current administrators were involved in the creation of the position?
- What are the expectations and goals for the position?
- Are these goals realistic based upon the information you have received?
- Was the position created due to a change in organizational culture?
- Was the position created due to a significant longstanding issue that needs to be resolved?
- Will the job experience prepare you for a better position in the future?

It is a good idea to continually review the organizational structure and politics even after accepting a leadership position. Before moving forward with a plan of action, I would suggest considering the following list of goals:

1. Peacefully co-exist with long-standing staff members and administrators.

2. Evaluate your organization's standard services and operations.

3. Evaluate your ability to enhance standard services and operations.

4. Produce quality work, but keep a low profile.

Choosing a New Business Vendor

Choosing a business vendor is a serious matter. In my opinion, the dynamic between a company and a vendor are similar to a close personal friendship or marriage. Trust and dependability are involved. A technology decision can make or break an organization. I view technology choices as two-year decisions that may last as long as five years. This type of decision naturally leads to requesting input from numerous staff members.

Here are the three types of questions involved when you are considering a technology decision:

1. Technology vendor questions

2. General business vendor questions

3. Political questions to privately consider

In some industries, the number of major and minor companies is constantly changing. As a manager, the decisions you make can drastically affect the existence of other companies.

<u>If you are attempting to choose a technology vendor, I would consider the following:</u>

- What kind of background do the people have who are heading up the new company?
- Can this new product or service affect the security of my position or industry?
- If so, why has the new product or service not already had an impact?
- How long will it take for the new idea to affect my position, organization, and/or industry?
- Does the idea or product make sense but lack industry support?
- If it makes sense, will people involved with the new idea or product end up being leaders in the industry?
- How long would it be before the new idea or product would be replaced?
- Is my industry ready to accept the new idea or product?

<u>Below is a list of general questions you may want to ask a potential business vendor:</u>

- May we have a brief organizational overview?
- What is your customer service approach for your current business partners?
- Do you have any plans to increase staffing in your customer service department?
- Are satisfaction surveys conducted with your current business partners?
- What successes did your organization experience during the past fiscal year?
- What challenges do you expect to face in the upcoming fiscal year?
- Can you update us on your goals for the upcoming fiscal year?
- For the upcoming fiscal year, are any new services or products available?
- What other companies, similar in size and scope to mine, do you currently serve?
- May we call a few of your current customers to discuss your products and services?

Again, selecting a business vendor is serious business. Many agreements are easy to cement and hard to dissolve.

<u>The last set of questions should be privately considered before you make a final decision:</u>

- Is a potential conflict of interest involved?

- Does the parent company of the potential vendor have a vested interest in me also using their other products?
- If so, are their other products up to the standards my organization requires?
- Does the potential business vendor have political connections involving upper administration in my organization?
- If so, will I truly be allowed to make the decision?

Chapter 2: Five Workplace Realities

Five common realities that are often overlooked when the term teamwork is being used are:

1. People's Careers Are Involved

2. Leaders Need to See the Big Picture

3. Some People Feel Overwhelmed by Life and Work

4. Some People Want Their Personal Needs Met at Work

5. You May Be Supervising Someone Who Applied For Your Current Position

Reality Number 1: People's Careers are Involved

How many times have you been told that there is no "I" in "team"? This is true, but the reality is that people's careers are involved. Corporate downsizing, layoffs, outsourcing, and scandals have totally

13

changed the sense of security Americans once had with their employers. When discussing the concept of teamwork, these realities come into play involving the duties, tasks, and assignments people are asked to perform. Competition among staff members is going to be involved.

Michelle Casto, in her book *Get Smart! About Modern Career Development*, identifies six stages of modern career development. They are Assessment, Investigation, Preparation, Commitment, Retention, and Transition. She believes that understanding the characteristics of each stage will empower people to navigate through them easily and with more confidence.

During the assessment and investigation stages, people are informally and formally asking questions about themselves and the world of work. In the preparation and commitment stage, the foundation for the first career is being set. The retention stage is when people are settled into a career and utilize a network to take advantage of other opportunities in the same field. The transition stage involves people being uncomfortable and unsure of the next steps to make. Eventually changes in the career of the individual involved will take place.

<u>Reality Number 2: Leaders Need to See the Big Picture</u>

Robert Kiyosaki, author of *Rich Dad Poor Dad*, makes this point by telling a story about a friend's

MBA class. In 1974, Ray Kroc, the founder of McDonalds, was the guest speaker for the friend's class. After the class, Kroc and the students went out to a local establishment. Kroc asked the students what business they thought he was in. The classmates laughed and had a good time as they thought that Kroc was joking. He asked the question again, and the laughter continued. Then one brave student said that everyone already knew he was in the hamburger business. Kroc informed them that he was not in the hamburger business, but that his business was real estate. Kroc went on to tell them that the prime locations where McDonalds restaurants are located are the main asset of his business. McDonalds is the largest single holder of real estate in the world. McDonalds also owns some of the most valuable intersections and street corners in America. I believe the point of the story is that looking beyond the surface and seeing the big picture is invaluable.

Reality Number 3: Some People Feel Overwhelmed by Life and Work

Based on my discussions with human resource officials at banks and universities and my own personal experiences, many people truly feel overwhelmed by life and work. Human resource officials are planning workshops about stress management, striking a work/life balance, and not taking everyday life so seriously. A few years ago I attended an office retreat facilitated by Dr. Tim Crowley. The retreat title was "How to Become an Extraordinary Team."

He also offered seven tips for developing your leadership potential which are listed below:

1. Love

2. Lighten Up

3. Stop Your "Stinking Thinking"

4. Adopt an Attitude of Gratitude

5. Live In the Present

6. Learn To Relax

7. Refresh

Along with many others, I enjoyed this workshop. My concern is for organizations that utilize only one type of leadership training. One approach will not better assist employees to learn about leadership or teamwork.

Reality Number 4: Some People Want Their Personal Needs Met at Work

Think about how many hours of the day you are involved with your daily duties and responsibilities. The reality is that a full-time employee spends most of his/her non-sleep hours on their job. This also translates into personal relationships being developed between people. Single, divorced, widowed, and married people have similar needs and wants. Some people would argue with me on this point, but people are generally the same. Yes, individual circumstances may dictate that people see one thing as more important than another. If their circumstances change, so will their thinking. This is why I conclude that people are basically the same.

Willard F. Harley Jr., in his book *His Needs, Her Needs, Building an Affair-Proof Marriage*, has identified 10 basic emotional needs. They are affection; sexual fulfillment; conversation; recreational companionship; honesty and openness; physical attractiveness of your partner; financial support; domestic support; family commitment; and admiration. If you think about these 10 needs, you will most likely recognize that you or someone you know has attempted to have one or more of these needs met at work.

Bishop T.D. Jakes, in his video series and book "The 10 Commandments of Working in a Hostile Work Environment," states that employees should not expect to be appreciated on the job. He also says that people should get their personal needs met at home. Jakes states that the expectation that you will be appreciated at work can lead to frustration. He says that the reality that people should be appreciated for what they do is separate from an expectation that they will be appreciated. A lot of it depends on the personality of your supervisor. I agree with him that employees cannot expect to have a supervisor who will appreciate them.

<u>Reality Number Five: You May Be Supervising Someone Who Applied for Your Current Position</u>

A limited number of supervisory positions are available in most organizations. Employees may informally prepare themselves to become a supervisor. The position they have been preparing for might be revamped, and the requirements could change. These types of decisions are normally only shared with members of the upper management team. Because a job candidate is not always aware of upper management's decisions, they can be utilizing a large number of assumptions to assist them to prepare for a higher-paying job. These factors can add to the feelings of disappointment if a long-time employee does not receive a promotion.

Upper management may view the pending retirement of a current supervisor as a chance to make major changes. An outside job candidate may be considered who might bring new ideas to the organization. In many situations, interview committees are considering this question: *Do we select a job candidate with many years of experience in our company, or do we consider an outside candidate that possesses the skill set needed to move us to the next level?*

Depending on your industry, other companies that hire people with your educational and work background may be in another state. Relocation may or may not be something you can or even want to consider. This and numerous other factors can make the dynamics involved in starting a new supervisory position very interesting.

If you are supervising a person who applied for your position, I offer the following recommendations:

Develop a Thick Skin - Do not take the situation personally. Not being offered a higher-paying job can cause a lot of emotions to be expressed in the workplace. If at all possible, take the high road when interacting with others.

Take Your Time Learning the Duties of the New Position - Don't become defensive, and don't try to make a positive impact too fast. Making a decision just because you can is a big management mistake. Relax and let yourself grow into the new position. You don't have to apply for the job you already have.

Invest in Your Own Personal Development - Consider taking college courses and/or continuing education classes. Ask yourself the question, "What can I do to better enhance my ability to do a good job?" Doing so will benefit you in your current and future career endeavors. Purchase a few management books.

Let Your Work Speak for You - Doing a good job speaks volumes. Remember that what you do will have more staying power than what you say.

Be Aware of Office Politics - Pay attention to who

the stakeholders are in your organization, but don't play office politics.

Enter Life's Classroom - Sometimes, an uncomfortable situation can prompt you to learn a valuable life lesson. For example, your job might help you identify how you handle stress. This can be a positive thing if you learn how to deal properly with the situation. Learn as much as you can from the current challenge.

Find Healthy Outlets Outside the Workplace - Exercise and other positive activities that can help you relax should be considered.

If You Make a Mistake, Own Up to It - It is impossible to know everything when you are in a new position. Not owning up to mistakes can cause bigger problems for you in the future.

Don't Attempt to Demand Respect; Remember, It is Earned – Treating others well and doing a good job are the best ways to earn respect.

Don't Take Yourself Too Seriously – Remember, your job is something you do, not who you are as a person.

If At All Possible, Only Leave For a Better Position - Do all you can to use this experience to enhance your job skills and advance your career. Don't be quick to leave the job due to a former job candidate being in the same office. Strive to keep moving forward.

Chapter 3: Building a Team

Being fair is important to gain the respect of the people you are leading. Although this is true, a family style of leadership is not the most effective. In a traditional family, the key is to provide a peaceful and loving atmosphere for the parents and children. Numerous everyday activities and annual events are scheduled to create bonding and a sense of unity. To the best of their ability, parents try to provide moral and/or spiritual training for their children. Family meetings may be held in which everyone votes on various topics. Parents may attempt to allow their unconditional love to create a safety net for their children. In this type of environment, children are provided an excellent opportunity to develop into positive and successful adults.

In a work setting, people from various backgrounds and walks of life are placed in the same environment. The ages and stages of their lives will vary. The reason people choose to, or have to, work also plays a factor in how people interact in the workplace. This makes an attempt to successfully implement a family-approach leadership style challenging. Even if this approach is used, it ties the hands of leadership. For example, if an employee needs to be written up, doing so is not consistent with creating a peaceful and loving atmosphere. I also believe some organizations have attempted to implement a family style of leadership under an approach called "team building."

In my opinion, true team building starts with everyone being hired, trained, developed, and released to utilize his or her skills to fulfill a specific role on the team. Employees are asked for their opinion regarding projects involving their daily work duties. No one team member is more important than anyone else. A true team approach allows leadership to handle employee problems fairly and to make final decisions, hopefully informed ones, involving organizational projects. Doing so is just part of a leader's role.

W. Steven Brown, in his book *13 Fatal Errors Managers Make and How You Can Avoid Them*, believes being "a buddy" and not a boss is a major problem. Two of the dynamics he describes are managing former peers and being a family, not a business. He found that a number of people struggle between being a buddy and being a boss if they are supervising a former peer. He suggests that upper management rid them of this temptation by having a supervisor removed from his or her former peers. This arrangement cannot always be made. If an employee must supervise former peers, Brown advises them to have a heart-to-heart discussion with his/her employee about the situation. This conversation should include both parties discussing how to properly deal with the new dynamics.

Brown also states that some small organizations or departments get away with a few years of buddy-buddy non-management, and then the organization or department increases the number of staff. Everyone attempts to tell the new employees what to do. If the person who was supposed to be managing the entire time decides to start doing so, everyone feels as though they have been demoted. He sees these organizations or departments as lacking the foundation for an organized expansion.

Jon R. Katzenbach, in his article "Making Teams Work at the Top," agrees with me that a true team clearly defines when input is appropriate and when it is not. He says that some organizations do not differentiate between or make a difference when team and non-team opportunities exist. He sees real teamwork as a potential benefit to an organization.

Patrick Lencioni, in his article "The Trouble with Teamwork," clearly identifies five dysfunctions commonly associated with teams.
These dysfunctions are:

■ Inattention to Results

■ Avoidance of Accountability

- Lack of Commitment

- Fear of Conflict

- Absence of Trust

He suggests that the following approaches can make a team become more successful:

1. Vulnerability-Based Trust - He sees this as the most important element of a good team. Team members must be willing to admit to their mistakes, weaknesses, and failures and when they need each other's help. Equally important is recognizing the strengths of others, even if they excel in an area that you struggle in. Lencioni states that this may seem easy on the surface and elementary to some people, but practicing this concept is difficult. Being vulnerable is not easy for a lot of leaders who have been taught to always be strong.

2. Healthy Conflict - Lencioni views a fear of conflict as a bad idea. Some leaders view conflict as a loss of control or a waste of time. He suggests that organizations identify artificial harmony and incite productive conflict in its place.

3. Unwavering Commitment - True teams need to make hard decisions and stick to them. If only part of a team is following the rules, this can cause infighting within an organization. He

makes the point that healthy conflict and commitment are not possible without trust.

4. Unapologetic Accountability - Great teams don't require the top leader to notify people when they are not pulling their own weight. Team members help other team members stay accountable. The goals of a team being clearly defined make this easier to do. Lencioni says that before deciding that teamwork is the answer to organizational challenges, the top leader of an organization should ask himself/herself and other top administrators the questions below:

- Can we keep our egos in check?
- Are we capable of admitting to mistakes, weaknesses, and insufficient knowledge?
- Can we speak up openly when we disagree?
- Will we confront behavioral problems directly?
- Can we put the success of the team or organization over our own?

If the answer to one or more of these questions is "probably not," then a group of top leaders should think twice about declaring themselves a team. Why? Because leaders set the tone for the organization.

Managing Versus Leading

When I think of managing, I think of a very busy workplace. Employees and supervisors are well aware of the immediate tasks at hand. Due to this situation, the goal is completing the tasks at hand and making it through the day. Supervisors assist with the various tasks assigned to their staff. They fill in as needed and keep an eye on other possible areas of need. Almost every organization goes through these types of stages. Busy times of the year, staff members getting ill, downsizing, etc. can all contribute toward these types of organizational experiences.

Supervisors assisting staff with a daily task is good for employee morale. Although this is true, an organization that stays in this type of situation is in a state of continual crisis. Managing is very task focused and sometimes crisis-driven. Leaders can effectively manage a crisis. Leadership involves taking things to the next level. You attempt to anticipate and prevent problems. Leaders lead by example and empower others to lead.

Successful leaders must have time to brainstorm and pre-plan. The best leaders are servants. Serving involves seeing the big picture and working toward accomplishing short and long-terms goals.

Chapter 4: Eight Teamwork Recommendations

Eight Recommendations to bring about True Teamwork are:

1. Attempt to See the Big Organizational Picture

2. Work on Listening Effectively

3. Remember that Other People's Careers are Also Involved

4. Make Ethical Organizational Decisions

5. Informally and Formally Study Successful Teams

6. Clearly Define Team and Non-Team Opportunities

7. Utilize a True Team Approach versus a Family Management Style

8. Strive to Keep a Healthy Work/Life Balance

1. Attempt to See the Big Organizational Picture

What is your organization's bottom line? How can you assist in helping them reach their goals? What is your organization's written mission statement? Does a true disconnect exist between what the mission statement says and what takes place in practice? If so, what is the unwritten mission statement? How can you assist with one or both of these missions being met? How does your position and department relate to your organization's core mission, or how does it relate to your organization's second or third level priorities?

These are the type of questions to review as you look beyond the surface issues within the organization to view the big organizational picture.

2. Work on Listening Effectively

It is important to understand the basics of human behavior when dealing with people. It is crucial for a person's opinion to be heard, and for him/her to be comfortable in their environment. How many times have you heard that children need structure and a routine in order to feel safe and secure? Well, it's the same for adults. If you have ever experienced a lot of organizational change yourself or have seen someone who has, you understand this truth. People, for the most part, do not like change. The lack of ethics and trust in some organizations may relate to people feeling this way.

At the same time, change in and of itself is difficult. These realities create a need to listen effectively and attempt to understand how a person has drawn a conclusion. You do not have to agree with someone's ideas, but it is good to attempt to understand their thought process. Fully listening to a person provides an opportunity to communicate what can be done about a concern, what cannot be done, and if talking about their concern will violate some level of confidentially involving another employee. It also provides the opportunity to communicate the timeline that has been established for the organization to deal with various challenges.

3. Remember that Other People's Careers are Also Involved

Success in an organization begins when you are given the opportunity to show others how you bring value to the table. In essence, it's about relationships. Without them, even the most skilled employee will not be given an opportunity to let their talent shine. I am not promoting that you attempt to be close to those in decision-making positions. Rather, I am offering a reminder of the need to work with others in a productive manner. Keep in mind that other people's careers are involved. There are some people who want to advance in their careers as well as those who are not interested in doing so.

Let's look at an example of a person who does not want career advancement. This individual is close to retirement and concerned about the number of pending changes before his last three years with the company. He has a lot of organizational history and positive things to contribute. At the same time, he does not want things to change and is in the way of progress that is needed in the next three to six months.

One management approach would be to wait until the person retires before progress is made. This is not always the best option, because three years of waiting until the staff member's retirement party may significantly affect the company's existence. If a direct interaction is needed due to this dynamic, an acknowledgement of current and past contributions to the company, along with the concern about the pending changes should be part of the conversation with the staff member. At the same time, the manager should request valuable input regarding how to make the changes, taking into account the person's institutional history while making it clear that change is needed and will take place. The staff member is then given an option to assist with the transition or to no longer play as significant of a role in future organizational decision making. This type of approach considers both the human feelings and the needs of the organization.

Another example involves someone who wants to advance his/her career. Unfortunately, not everyone can move up without looking for and accepting an opportunity outside of the organization. Due to this reality, staff members should evaluate reasons to stay with an organization or consider other options every two to five years. Numerous personal and professional reasons will contribute to how this decision is made. The most important thing is approaching the process in a methodical and intelligent manner. Doing so can eliminate all or some levels of feeling bitter or being stuck. Sometimes a person may be truly stuck. If so, considering outside activities like consulting or a side business are good ways to reassert some control over your situation.

4. Make Ethical Organizational Decisions

The importance of ethics cannot be stressed enough. It is the solid foundation upon which other things are built. Yet being ethical in and of itself does not equal being a good leader. Some people with good ethics may not be good at serving others in an organization or may not understand the current challenges facing your organization or industry. A company may go out of business or become ineffective if a clear and proper business vision is not in place. Some organizations may settle for an ethical leader without vision in the top position due to a past scandal involving an executive. Having proper checks and balances in place is one of numerous effective ways to deal with this concern. Enforcement of the rules involving the checks and balances is also important. People are quick to understand what the rules say and how they are followed in practice. Also, having a diverse leadership team that consists of people with various talents is vital to the success of any organization. No one person has the skill set to effectively lead an entire team.

5. Informally and Formally Study Successful Teams

Media stories are aired on a regular basis involving top professional sports coaches and business executives. The leadership approach used by the coach or executive is the highlight of the story. A look behind the scenes will reveal assistant coaches and vice president level staff who are doing a great job involving specific departments within the organization. In the sports arena, assistant coaches of successful teams are regularly considered by team owners to take on a head coaching position. In the business world, some executives have to sign non-compete agreements. This is partially due to the company knowing the employee has the potential and exposure to decrease the parent company's profit margin. The person signing this agreement is an important part of the team.

In the business world, when you get below the executive level, this lesson is sometimes lost. Sometimes frontline staff ideas and input are not valued. If this takes place, a great opportunity to advance the organization is being missed. If an organization oversells and under delivers a product to a customer, it may decrease or eliminate future orders. Frontline staff members have the ability to provide input to prevent this negative dynamic.

6. Clearly Define Team and Non-Team Opportunities

Every team decision should be well thought out with the best interests of the organization and individuals in mind. No decision should be made without at least asking those directly involved in the process how things really work. Doing so will allow staff members to see the complexity and thought that goes into the decision making process. At the same time, all decisions should not be made by committee. If a decision does not warrant a committee-type vote but instead requires input from others, a clear communication explaining the dynamics involved is needed. Some committees and boards use words like "advisory" and "oversight," which do not set clear boundaries and effectively communicate the role of the group. Part of the problem, in some cases, is an unclear mission statement or charge for group members.

Let's look at a not-for-profit organization as an example. The mission of the board of directors and the mission statement may relate to a need to provide services to the local community. In practice, the agency director's duties and that of the board is to raise funds to assist in providing additional services for the community. No need really exists for the agency director and the board of directors to micromanage the day-to-day activities of the social workers doing the hands-on work. If this is not clearly defined or understood, then numerous unneeded memos and rules to inform the social workers how to directly serve the public tend to be produced. The result is business executives who compose the board with no training in social work that micromanage dedicated social workers with graduate-school level training in social work. That is why the roles on a team must be clearly defined for the success of any organization.

7. Utilize a True Team Approach versus a Family Management Style

An effective team comprises talented people who know their roles and work toward meeting a common goal. Trust is involved, as is accountability to each other and the common goals. It takes hard work to get a team to this point, but the effort is worth it. The team leaders need to continue to remind themselves of the importance of not crossing the line between personal friendships and being the team leader. This also comes down to a matter of definition of the word "friendship." When a person is leading their team effectively without playing favorites and understands the true definition of a friendship, this will not become an issue for the organization.

True friendship involves trust, accountability, and open discussions about issues as they come up. Confusion takes place when people are not clear about the definition of friendship or confuse it with being a situational comrade. A situational comrade dynamic takes place when people share the same goals or experiences for a period of time. A feeling of closeness is present due to the common experience. Working for the same organization or taking a college class together would be two examples. The key is seeing if the bond goes beyond this common experience or if both people have each other's best interests at heart. If a team member has the team leader's best interests at heart, he/she would not want to ask for or accept favors that would affect the leader's ability to lead the team. The opposite is also true. A team leader with the best interests of the team member in mind would not want to put someone in a position to not be able to interact with other members of the team in an effective manner. A team approach puts the best interests of everyone involved first.

8. Strive to Keep a Healthy Work/Life Balance

This topic is discussed in the media on a regular basis. Reflecting upon your own personality and how you approach life is important when reviewing this subject. One of the most essential issues for a person to reflect upon is who they are. Every person has different skill sets and contributions to make to the world. Knowing who you are and your place in the world makes such a key difference to how you approach life. The work environment you prefer and how you are or are not taking care of your health and why are important, too.

A person's attitude regarding wellness and spiritual questions is also something to think about. You will come to a point in your career (or may already be at that point) at which you feel more demand for your work hours. You may also be considering or already taking care of your aging parents. If you are younger, your time away from work may be balanced with starting a family. The excitement you may feel about increased career opportunities can become mixed with a concern about how to balance your personal and professional life.

Related to leading a team, the key question is how these things affect your leadership style and effectiveness. It is important to remember that leaders do their best if they are taking care of themselves. Striking a balance between your personal and professional life is the key. Balance does not result in all things in a person's life being seen as equal or warranting the same time commitment, but it does create a sense of how to have enough time for all the activities in your life and how to really enjoy them and the time you spend with others.

Conclusion

A true understanding of teamwork will not come about by becoming familiar with one management school of thought. Instead, a formal and informal evaluation of leadership information and real life examples are needed to result in a well rounded and increased knowledge base. Looking beyond the obvious and really wanting to utilize teamwork is a worthy goal. The results of all of your hard work will have a lasting impact. Leadership of any organization starts at the top. If a leader is not being honest about his/her personal challenges, the entire organization can be affected. I suggest that every leader privately consider asking him/herself the following questions in an attempt to remain accountable:

- How important is my organizational role to how I view myself as a person?
- What type of work environment do I prefer?
- What type of tasks do I prefer?
- How can my leadership style lead to my success?

- How can my leadership style lead to my failure?
- Am I getting regular health check-ups?
- Am I getting enough sleep at night?
- Are my eating habits OK?
- Do I have any personal, family, or other relationship issues that I have not dealt with?
- Am I attempting to have my personal needs met at work?
- Does it bother me to make unpopular decisions?
- Is so, how am I dealing with these types of dynamics?
- Is the spiritual and self-care part of my life healthy?
  - How are my time management skills?

Over the past 14 years, I have been involved in numerous teambuilding exercises that have exposed me to a variety of experiences. Most of these sessions seemed to not even come close to dealing with real workplace issues. When these sessions were really bad, I could not wait until it was time to get back to some regular day-to-day work.

Some people I know have totally bought into the concepts discussed at these types of training sessions. When they attempt to apply what was learned to the realities of the workplace, I have seen people begin to not to trust the motives or intent of the training. The research I conducted concludes that most organizations do not have an alternative agenda when offering a training workshop. Some organizational leaders truly believe that you can build a team only utilizing a teambuilding workshop approach. Also, some people are so stressed out by life that they are eager to receive and provide such relief to others. This is not a criticism but the reality of the pressures and demands of modern life. How many people have informally or formally studied leadership? Most managers I know do not read management books at all or only read motivational-type business books. Based on my discussions with numerous bookstore managers, these motivational books are the most popular. I believe the reason for that is the important role that hope plays in every-one's life.

Hope is a key component to success. At the same time, a person needs specific instructions on how to proceed once inspired. Another thing I discovered was that most management books fall into the fol-lowing 12 categories:

1. Business Fiction – Real workplace challenges are dealt with in a story format.

2. Motivational – General and helpful reminders are provided encouraging the reader to believe in him/herself and not give up.

3. Motivational and Practical Application – These types of books do offer a little more specific practical application material.

4. Research Based/Practical Application – Prestig-

ious college and university presses publish these types of books.

5. Ethics – These books remind us that ethics are the solid foundation upon which things are built.

6. Autobiography – Famous business people offer advice based on their personal experiences.

7. Fight the System – Books reminding people to take their career into their own hands are in this category.

8. Back to Basics – Asking people to consider the wisdom and insights of years past is involved.

9. Military Style – Using military ideas to effectively run a business and become more successful are discussed.

10. Gender/Race Issues – Career advice specifically geared toward women and minorities is offered.

11. Practical Application – Non-research-based general leadership or management advice is involved.

12. Academic – Textbooks for management courses are in this category.

I talked to a number of authors from the 12 leadership and management philosophical camps. It is interesting to note that most of them are dedicated to their philosophical camp. Some crossing of camps exists between the ethics and practical application areas and there is a little overlap between academic and practical application.

This has also caused me to look more closely at the endorsements on the back of books. In most cases, the endorsement is from someone in the same philosophical camp. In order for a manager to gain a well-rounded view of teamwork, he/she must read and consider the ideas and views of people in different philosophical camps. Don't always select the next book you are going to read because it was recommended by the author of the book you just finished.

While true teamwork is hard to accomplish, if achieved, great benefits and outcomes can be the result. Organizational leaders need to consider various teamwork concepts and decide which ones are best to implement in their organization.

References

Maxwell, J. (2003). There's No Such Things As "Business" Ethics. New York, NY: Grand Central Publishing (formerly Warner Books).

Covey, S. (1998). The Seven Habits of Highly Effective People. New York, NY: Simon and Schuster.

Casto, M. (2000). Get Smart! About Modern Career Development. Corpus Christi, Texas: Get Smart Publishing.

Kiyosaki, R. and Lechter, S. (1998). Rich Dad Poor Dad. New York, NY: Grand Central Publishing (formerly Warner Books).

Harley, W. (2001). His Needs, Her Needs: Building An Affair Proof Marriage. Ada, Michigan: Fleming H. Revell Company.

Harley, W. (2004). Emotional Needs. http://www.marriagebuilders.com
Crowley, T. (2004). Dr. Tim Crowley: Speaker - Author - Trainer.

McGhee, K. (2003). Eleven Leadership Tips For Supervisors. Charleston, South Carolina: Booksurge Publishing.

Jakes, T.D. (2002). The 10 Commandments of Working in a Hostile Work Environment (Video Series). Dallas, Texas.

Jakes, T.D. (2005). The 10 Commandments of Working in a Hostile Work Environment.
New York, N.Y. Berkley Hardcover.

Brown, W. (1985). 13 Fatal Errors Managers Make and How You Can Avoid Them. New York, NY: Berkley Publishing.

Lencioni, P. (2003). The Trouble with Teamwork.
http://www.pfdf.org/leaderbooks/l2l/summer2003/lencioni.html

Katzenbach, J (1998). Making Teams Work at the Top.
http://www.leadertoleader.org/knowledgecenter/L2L/winter98/katzenbach.html

About the Author

Kenneth McGhee has extensive experience in training college, university and high school staff members and presenting at the state and national level. Numerous media outlets have quoted him about management, career and technology issues including the Chicago Tribune, Baton Rouge Business Report, Monster.com, Web Host Industry Review Magazine (Canada) and Insight CPA Magazine. McGhee earned his undergraduate degree from the University of Alabama at Birmingham and obtained his graduate degree from Northern Illinois University.

Contact Information:
teamworkbook@yahoo.com